Here we are again at
number 3 Tree Street.
Time for all good chimps to get up.

Look, here comes Mash with a cup on his head.

That's what comes of going to Miss Twinkletoes' Charm School for Chimps. "No more tea for you in bed," says Mum.

They'll have just a quick snack
for breakfast.
It's bananas on toast and a cup of tea.

Oh dear, Mum has left the teapot
on the table.
It looks tempting. No, Bangers, don't!

They are having a smashing time
this morning.
"No pocket money for a month," says Dad.

No pocket money for a month.
They do look sad on the school bus.

Mrs Chum is waiting for them.
Well, she looks happy anyway.

She has a pottery wheel, a kiln and a
great pile of sticky, red clay.
They're in luck! They can make a teapot
and two cups for Mum.

Just a minute, Mrs Chum, do you think
you should let them?
Think about the chimps and sticky,
red clay.

There's Petal making a cup.
Doesn't she look sweet?

There's Bangers.
No, he's not fooling about, he's getting the air out of the clay.

Oh dear, the phone is ringing.
Mrs Chum has got to leave the chimps.
Do you think she should?

Oh dear, Petal is making the wheel go
as fast as she can.
Clay is all over Mash.

Bangers! Don't paddle in the clay bin.
You'll have feet of clay.

Thank goodness! Here comes Mrs Chum
back from the phone.
They must do their ABC ten times.

It's time to glaze the pots.
No, glaze the pots, not your arms, Mash.

It's time to take the pots out of the kiln.
I say, that teapot has five spouts.

Those cups look like big milk jugs.
Never mind, I hope they get them home
safely on the bus.

Here they are back again at
number 3 Tree Street.
I think we had better look in on their tea.

There they all are sitting round the table.
And Dad has given Bangers and Mash
their pocket money.

Mum is so proud of them.
Look she is going to pour out the tea.

Yes, it works!
You can pour out five cups at once.
Well, it almost works . . .

That's what I call a real feat.
It's a real feat of clay.